90-Day Fiancé: *Bittersweet Memories*

First Edition

ISBN 978-1-387-74417-6

Dantes Joseph

Margate, Florida 33063

USA

INTRODUCTION

The purpose of this book is to share a very personal experience with the 90-day fiancé visa offered in the **United States** *(U.S.)*. The program allows non-immigrants to temporarily come to the U.S. for a period of 90 days to marry their citizen fiancé. After the marriage, the foreign spouse can apply for adjustment of status and receive a conditional two-year green card. Conditional, because they have to prove that the marriage was genuine. If the couple is still together after two years, they must follow up with an interview at the **U.S. Citizenship and Immigration Services** *(USCIS)*. If all goes well, the spouse can now receive a green card valid for ten years.

To protect identities, I'll only be using the first or nicknames of the people involved. Throughout the book, I'll provide information about the visa process. But the focus, is not about the process; it's on the **bittersweet** experience *Aileen* and I went through. The relationship with the woman I married had some good memories. But it also had considerable challenges that I think are worth sharing.

For Your Information: In this book, the word Fiancé with a single *(é)* refers to either male or female. All currency is in *U.S. dollars*. And the colored phrases throughout the book, highlight all the reasons that eventually lead to the bitter part of this story.

CHAPTER 1: SWEET MEETING

Filipino Cupid

You may already be familiar with the site filipinocupid. This is where *Aileen* and I first met. I've been divorced since early 1994 and have had some casual relationships. I was browsing the site, as I tend to find Filipino women attractive with a culture similar to mine. American women, in my view, are more liberated. Being in the U.S. can make them lose sight of their blessings. I was looking for someone conservative with old-fashion values. I was born in Haiti and came to the U.S. at the age of eleven. I'm a naturalized citizen who grew up in upstate New York and New Jersey. When I met Aileen online I was 53 and she was 45.

We began to chat on August 11th 2015. At that time, she seemed to have a low self esteem about some of her physical features. For that she tried to avoid video chats. But once we did have a video chat on Facebook, I thought she was attractive. Of course on camera it's not always easy to fully analyze a person. But I found that in addition to her posture, she had a sense of humor. I also liked her personality. She seemed to understand me and was attracted to me as well.

We've had some light arguments as we were getting to know each other. One night I was angry about something she said or did. And after some remarks I ended the conversation. But she was resilient and kept calling back. I picked up once, but it was late and I told her I wanted to get some sleep. I woke up in the middle of the night and she was still calling. I thought it was a bit strange and flattering at the same time. To me, it was unusual that someone would spend a good part of the night by the phone wanting to make up. But despite the occasional spats we continued to chat almost on a daily basis. I was impressed how good of a dancer *Aileen* is. We had some good times as we listened to songs and danced together on video. We continued chatting for about six months.

Off To The Philippines

In order to begin the fiancé visa, the law requires for the couple to have met <u>in person</u> within a two-year period, prior to the petition. And since *Aileen* had never step foot in the U.S., you guessed it! I had to find the time and money to be with her in the Philippines.

Before the trip, I thought about the moments when *Aileen* would show a bitter side of her. Sometimes it would be a jealous reaction to a couple of Filipino women I was chatting with before AND during my chats with her. On Facebook, if another Filipina liked or commented on my pictures, *Aileen* would post comments like "He is MY boyfriend!" I would either remove her comments or she would later delete them. I began to pick up on her jealousy and mentioned it to a couple of her friends as I hesitated to continue chatting with her. I told them that *Aileen* is ***napaka-selosa***; Tagalog for "very Jealous." While *Aileen* would admit her jealousy, she claimed it's because she really loves me.

I had made arrangements for the trip, but towards the end I got cold feet. So without telling her, I cancelled the plane and hotel reservation. The cancellation cost me about $500. But Even though I realized that going there could be a mistake, I also thought it was unfair to her. I was looking forward to the trip and said to myself "worst-case scenario" I'd make a vacation out of it. One of my sisters reminded me that I needed a getaway. So in a chat later that day, I told *Aileen* I was having second thoughts and had canceled the trip. Of course, she was hurt and began to cry. Seeing it was a mistake, I became a bit emotional and apologized. I thought spending time with her could be refreshing, after all.

I asked her not to give up on me and started looking for another flight. I wanted to make the most of the trip by traveling on Emirates Airlines even though I knew it was more expensive. Lucky for me, I found another bargain, on Emirates where the round-trip ticket was $1,300. About an extra $200 from the first reservation, but still cheaper than its regular flights. A typical round-trip flight on Emirates to the Philippines could cost over $2,000. You can also find some good deals if you book the reservation online.

On January 21, 2016 I embarked on that long journey to meet my potential future wife☐. I flew on JetBlue for about three hours from Florida to New York. From there, I got on Emirates for about a 12-hour flight to Dubai. From Dubai, I got on another Emirates flight that got me to Manila close to eight hours later. It was a *looong* flight! Halfway around the world to be exact. I also had to deal with the twelve-hour time difference. Before the trip, I had also booked a hotel room at Capital Towers, through **Airbnb** which was a short walk from where *Aileen* was staying on E. Rodriguez Ave. The room was on the 29nd floor with a nice view of *Makati City*.

At the airport in the Philippines, I have to admit that at first, I was a little disappointed when I saw *Aileen*. I knew she had a facial skin pigmentation called ***Melasma***, but didn't know how different it would make her look in person. She tried to hide it by putting something on her face a few days before which, I think, made it worse. The stuff she put on made it look like her skin was peeling off. Also, without going into too much detail, I was a little taken back by her teeth when she smiled. So needless to say, it wasn't one of those moments of running into each other's arms. *Aileen* is also *petite;* About 110 pounds and close to 5 feet tall. She had told me that she doesn't consider herself sexy or pretty. Sometimes she'd say **Pangit ako, at Maganda sila** *"I'm ugly; the others are prettier than me."* She has a little more boobs than booty and somewhat less than good measurements. In fact I tease her sometimes that she has a stomach pouch that takes away from a more sexy waistline. But overall, I think she does have enough to satisfy someone like me.

I was not too impressed with her living environment; but then I expected that to some degree. She lived in a squatter alleyway where homes are scrunched together. Towards the back of the alley, near her entrance, was an unpleasant trash-like smell that was noticeable but not completely unbearable. We had to go up two flights of steep and dangerous stairs to reach her bedroom. Once, she accidentally fell down the first set of stairs and got a few nasty bruises. At some point, though, I began to question whether I should even be there! "Maybe I made a mistake; Is this the best I could do?" I thought to myself. But as mentioned previously I am from Haiti. And although I have not lived under the same conditions, I was familiar with them and people who've lived in them.

But despite the first impression, I never lost sight of the features that first attracted me to *Aileen*: some of her facial expressions, when she talks, reminds me of two of the most loved ones in my life: First my belated brother *Philippe* and my younger son *Erick*. In fact even today, despite any flaws, this is one of *Aileen*'s most dominant features to me. And her voice! There's something about her facial expression and baby-like voice that bring about a certain weakness in me. So what I liked about her somehow outweighed her flaws. The problem though is how SHE feels about herself; the insecurity she sometimes carries around.

For me, even these conditions are not a deciding factor. I've had relationships with women who were better off financially. And yet I never got along with them for a variety of other reasons. So I don't really care if someone is rich or poor. What I am concerned with is the condition of the heart. I was looking for humility, honesty and trust. My ideal woman doesn't have to be Miss Universe; but everyone appreciates a pretty face and a nice body to match, if at all possible. By the way, *Aileen* is not ugly. In fact the more I got to know her, the more I picked up on her token beauty. One, I think, will always be with her.

Spending Time In Manila

The overall stay was nice. And although we didn't go to any fancy places or did anything extravagant, we had fun learning about each other's customs. We went to the beach, the mall, ice skating, some parks and fast-food places like *Jollibee*. We spent some time at her place but she pretty much stayed with me at the hotel. We travelled to Biñan to visit more of *Aileen*'s family. *Aileen* can be playful: she would sometimes knock on the front door and then run and hide. She has a child-like attitude that I felt comfortable with. *Aileen* was super nice and attentive to my needs. She would hold on dearly to my arm when we walked on the streets and take *jeepneys* together.

When I first got to the Philippines I rented a car, hoping to be able to ride around quicker and in more comfort. But traffic there was rough! In Haiti also, driving is like survival of the fittest. But the Philippines, I think, is worse. If you're not used to driving in a third-world country, I wouldn't recommend it. In fact there was a time *Aileen* and I, along with her nephew **Willy** went to the *Mall of Asia*. On the way there, a policeman stopped me and said that I was changing lanes without signaling. That wasn't true, of course. In fact, compared to the other drivers, I was one of the more cautious ones. I suspected he pulled me over because I looked like a tourist; one who could offer him money to get out of a ticket situation. He said he was going to take away my license and I'd have to go to the station and pay a fee to get it back. Of course, we didn't have time for all that. *Aileen* talked to him and I ended up giving him about $13 cash I had in my wallet. Soon after, I realized it would be safer and more economical to use public transportation. So a couple of days later, *Aileen* and I drove downtown to return the car. She was very useful and patient as she waited for me for almost an hour. I was also looking into investing in a pre-construction condo project named **Kasara**, at one time. There again *Aileen* would wait quietly for as long as it took when we visited the models and when I was negotiating. Occasionally she would offer some input; but was always OK with whatever I decided.

Aileen's family and friends were very nice and friendly. We sang karaoke, they offered me gifts, they cooked for me and made me feel welcome. I should also add that I was yet to get used to Filipino food. Especially the rice they cook with no salt! But I liked a certain *coffee bread Aileen* used to buy at a nearby bakery. We'd have it with breakfast early mornings near the window, on that 29th floor of the hotel room. I had no reason to distrust *Aileen* nor her family and friends, even when it came to money. Her brother-in-law **Joey** who was staying in the same house as *Aileen* was extremely caring. Even when I offered to pay for things when we'd go out, he would insist on picking up the tab. He used to bring a certain gadget, to the hotel room, that gave *Aileen* and I access to a lot movies. When it comes to money he was very generous. In fact I came to trust *Aileen* just the same. And her perception of *Joey* was one of trust. She would often point out the people she thought were less trustworthy. But she had a very good and trusting relationship with *Joey*.

Before we returned the rental car, there was a very nice security guard outside the Hotel name **Abbad**. He'd always reserve us a parking space when we return to the Hotel. *Aileen* would ask me "how much should we give *Abbad*?" I thought it was a sweet reminder on her part and we became good friends with *Abbad* in the process.

But just as we had some fights in the chats, we did have an argument here and there. I witnessed some war-of-words *Aileen* had with one of her sisters about another sister who lives in Canada. There, I noticed she can get very angry. Even more of concern was the jealousy she displayed when she saw a friend she thought I had deleted on Facebook. That became increasingly troubling when she expressed jealousy over two other Filipinas that I was chatting with before AND during the time *Aileen* and I were talking. On Facebook, she monitored who my friends are. She felt threatened by these Filipinas to the extent she kept asking me to delete them. I told her that deleting would not stop me from chatting with them if I wanted to. I guess in her mind, they would wonder why I deleted them and no longer talk to me? That seemed to make sense; and in fact that's what happened: I deleted them to please Aileen. I didn't think it was necessary and it just showed me again that she was insecure and didn't trust me.

When I first got to the Philippines, I casually mentioned that maybe I should visit one or two of my friends. One was *Sophie* who lived in Cebu. Keep in mind that *Aileen* and I had not committed to anything. My trip was to visit the Philippines. And in doing so, I would fulfill the requirements needed to begin a fiancé visa. So I thought, why not? I am a long way from home and maybe I should not put all my eggs in one basket. I could visit another friend in case things didn't work out with *Aileen*. Now I only mentioned "possibly" going to Cebu as part of my trip. But I had no formal plans of doing it. The thought of sightseeing and saying *hi* to someone I chatted with online, to me was innocent. The other was *Marlene* who lived in Manila. But I didn't know exactly where and had not previously talked to her about my visit.

Anyway, since my trip was focused around *Aileen*, I dropped the thought of meeting other friends or going to Cebu. That would have eaten into the time I came to spend in Manila anyway; not to mention the additional cost of the plane ticket to Cebu, which is about an hour's flight south of Manila. But just the fact that I mentioned it drove *Aileen* crazy. To this day, she often reminds me of how I wanted to visit my "girlfriends" in the Philippines. Maybe she had a point!

Stick-To-The-Plan

The time for me to leave Manila was getting closer and *Aileen* began to give me a sad look☹. I felt bad about leaving her in the same conditions, when I know she wanted to be with me. She calls me **Mahal** which is Tagalog for *Love*. She was saying to me *Sasama ako sayo!* Tagalog for "I'll come with you!" I should also mention she proposed that we get married in the Philippines. Of course I didn't think it was a good idea. First of all, I didn't go there to get married and second, I wasn't familiar with their marriage laws. From what I understand, this is a country where divorce is illegal. Not that I had divorce in mind, but we were still in courtship.

Previously I've questioned whether *Aileen* was motivated to work. The impression I got, was that she appeared to be lazy; thinking she may only be interested in a visa for her and her daughter who was

eighteen at the time. *Aileen* would find some care-giving jobs every now and then, but they were usually short lived. She was picky and always had a reason for turning down jobs or not sticking to them for long. She used to receive money from her sister in Canada, mostly for caring for the sister's teenage son, *Willy*. *Willy* has since gone to be with his mother in Canada. *Aileen* was living rent free with *Willy* and *Willy*'s father *Joey*. So my concern was that this could give *Aileen* a lack of desire to provide for herself.

I was also worried about her appearance since she wasn't physically active. But in all fairness, I learned that she was anemic which would make her weak at times and could explain her lack of strength or desire to work. She told me she wasn't too interested in working in Manila, but was willing to work in the U.S. The U.S., is the land of opportunity, that's true. But there are those who think that opportunity is just handed to you. When it comes to working, this is a very competitive country. Of course I would be there for support; but the plan was for her to first take advantage of opportunities in Manila and in the long run be able to help provide for the family she would be leaving behind.

So considering all the above, I came up with the phrase *stick-to-the-plan*. I offered encouragement by telling her that until I petition for her, I'd like to see that she occupies her mind by working. And if she works, she should save her money since she had little obligation in her current living arrangements. I also tried to encourage her to exercise a little to lose some of that stomach pouch. I thought she might feel better about herself if she could address the things she didn't like about her body.

Leaving Manila

As I said, everyone was super nice and made sure my needs were met all the way to the airport. *Aileen* packed my bags and we caught a taxi together with her brother-in-law *Joey*. We had enough time before the flight so we stopped at a fast-food joint, at the airport, for a bite. And *Joey* was thoughtful enough, again, to pick up the tab.

When it came time for me to go to the gate, *Joey* went to wait outside while *Aileen* and I said goodbye. She told me not to forget her and said that no one has ever cared for her like me.
Unlike when I first arrived, this goodbye was emotional and tearful. We got to know and trust each other a little more with my visit. I told her I was not planning on forgetting her; even though I was still wrestling with some of the concerns I previously had. But I was also sad, knowing that she's come to depend on me and, once again, we were going to be miles apart. Finally we said goodbye and agreed to **stick-to-the-plan**. And after a 21 day-visit in Manila, I embarked, once again, on a 20+ hours of flight to Florida.

The Petition

When I got back, I took the time to reflect on the trip. And despite some of the negative feelings I had towards *Aileen*, I began to miss the trip and the good times we had. But I was still undecided on whether or not to call her. I knew if I didn't, she would be really upset. In fact, at the airport before I came back, *Joey* asked me if they would ever see me again. It's like he and *Aileen* thought that once I left, that would be it; especially when *Aileen* was already afraid that I wouldn't like her.

Being alone again and back to the same routine, I felt the need for company. I call this the *point of no return!* I had to distinguish between compassion and a real desire to be with her. At this point we had built some emotion between us and any attempt to turn away from it could be painful. But it is the best time to turn away if your heart tells you NOT to commit. It's usually hard for me to say NO especially if it means hurting someone. I weighed the pros and cons and asked myself if I'd be OK following up with the relationship. Knowing, also that I still had time to decide on marriage, I called her and she was very excited to hear from me.

I filed the petition for *Aileen* in the beginning of May, 2016. The way it works is that you first have to apply for your fiancé with the *USCIS* on form I-129F. If the petition is approved, it's sent to the National Visa Center, who will process and forward it to the U.S. Embassy or consulate nearest your fiancé's residence. They will then invite him or her to apply for the visa. At the time I filed, the cost was $340. And as naïve as I was, I thought that was it. I thought that was the cost of the application that would take about six months to approve and then I'd just buy a ticket for *Aileen*. Boy was I wrong!

In the petition, you must show that you are (a) a U.S. citizen (b) you and your fiancé intend to marry within 90 days of them entering the U.S. (c) you're both free to marry and (d) you've met each other in person within two years prior to filing. There are two exceptions to the two-year meeting: (1) if it would violate strict and long-established customs of you or your fiancé's foreign culture or social practice and (2) if you can prove that the requirement to meet your fiancé would result in extreme hardship to you.

Aileen and I had already met, so we were good to go with the petition. It included the I-129F form along with two recent passport photos, for me, and an accompanying G-325A *(Biographic Information)*. It's basically a résumé showing all the places you've lived and worked for the recent five years. A separate copy is needed for each of you. At the time of filing, you also need a Form I-134 *(Affidavit of Support)*. But don't worry too much about this one. It's for informational purposes and is not really considered. Once your fiancé is in the U.S and you're ready to change his or her status, you will be required to sign another, more important, affidavit of support which I discuss later.

The petition also included a **Statement of Intent to Marry**. But they don't hold you accountable if the marriage doesn't take place. It's a short letter you can put together stating that you are petitioning for your fiancé abroad. And once in the U.S., you intend to marry within the 90-day period. Your fiancé will need to draft and sign one also. The petition I submitted was ultimately approved and I received a Notice of Action, form I-797 showing a receipt date of May 12, 2016 and a notice date of September 8, 2016. So about four months later, the petition was approved and was valid through January 7, 2017.

Aileen's Interview

Once accepted your petition is sent to the *National Visa Center*. We had to pay another application fee along with DS-160 form *(non-immigrant visa application)*. It can also be submitted online at **ceac.state.gov/genniv/**. The fee at the time was about $255. It had to be deposited at a bank in the Philippines where we were given a receipt number that had to be recorded with the form.

In addition, *Aileen* had to get police clearances. In her case she needed clearances both from the Filipino government as well as from the *United Arab Emirates (UAE)* where she had previously worked for a number of years. So you can imagine how difficult it was since she would have to know someone there or go herself to take care of it. Good thing she had a trusted friend working there. He took time off his busy schedule and did the legwork in getting the clearance. *Aileen* had her brother-in-law *Joey* secure the clearance she needed in the Philippines. Another hurdle she had to overcome was to contact an attorney regarding an error on her belated boyfriend's death certificate. It seemed to suggest that they were married. So, although not much, that's additional cash she had to spend to clear up that issue.

Aileen had to gather all this paperwork to prepare for her interview at the U.S. Embassy. She also had to go for a medical exam where they usually check your physical and mental health, blood work and vaccinations. The results of the exam are passed to the U.S. Embassy for review. In some cases, the physician forwards them and in other cases, the applicant brings the results to the interview. Once you set a date for the interview, you'll be instructed to schedule the exam with an approved physician. Conveniently, *Aileen* lived close to a medical center and was able to set an appointment there. She had some money set aside for the exam which cost about $245. At the medical office, you should bring the following:

- Vaccination records
- Previous medical history *(surgeries, medications, possible hospitalizations, etc.)*

- Passport as proof of ID *(or other acceptable forms)*
- Visa interview confirmation letter
- Payment *($245 in our case)*
- There may be other requirements listed in the packet.

There are three parts to the exam, but they're normally done the same day:

- Questionnaire
- Chest X-ray
- Physical examination and blood test

The above is just a summary of what I remember about the process. You should not solely rely on this information since it may change from time to time.

Thankfully *Aileen* came clean with her results. A question people ask is if they test you for *Sexually Transmitted Diseases (STDs)*. There was a test for Gonorrhea but not for *Acquired Immune Deficiency Syndrome (AIDS)*. Speaking of AIDS, *Aileen* and I had had the conversation. We figured with marriage, we should both be tested. We were supposed to do it during my visit to the Philippines but somehow we kept putting it off. I knew I was OK because it had been a while since I was sexually active. *Aileen* was also confident she was OK for pretty much the same reason. Although we thought that once she comes to the U.S., we could follow up on it just for the peace of mind. I suggested that since she was doing the other exams, it might be a good idea if she got tested also. But I wasn't going to hold her to it because I didn't want her to feel despised. And God forbid if there was a problem, we'd be facing a tough decision about whether or not to continue the process. But one day she surprised me by telling me she'd gotten the HIV test. Thankfully again, her results were good.

Once we paid for the application at the National Visa Center *(NVC)*, obtained the police clearances and medical report, *Aileen* was finally ready for the interview. That's her sitting down with an examiner at the U.S. Embassy and going through the questions on the application. One important task is for the examiner to make a judgment call on possible visa fraud. A big age difference between the petitioner and the fiancé, for example, could be a problem. They would also ask questions about our first meeting in the Philippines. I suspect they also want to see to what the extent the fiancé speaks English. While he or she doesn't have to be fluent, being able to answer questions without a translator is a plus. They would have also asked *Aileen* questions that showed how well she knows me. By the way, I was able to complete the DS-160 for *Aileen*, online. But they do ask that the fiancé abroad do the electronic signing.

Aileen did OK on the interview but they followed up with an unexpected task: they wanted to see ALL of our text messages from Facebook Messenger. I thought that was crazy! We'd been chatting on a daily basis for almost a year. I tried to select certain chats that didn't include any nasty language or arguments. But after doing this twice, they continued to ask for ALL the chats. *Aileen* became frustrated and thought about quitting. But being organized, she bought an Album and put pictures with related comments together with all her paperwork. She got a friend with access to a computer to print the remaining chats. After that, her visa was approved. At the interview they asked her to bring a valid passport with an expiration date at least six months beyond the 90-day limit in the U.S. She also needed recent passport pictures and the visa was stamped in the passport. At that point you can either have the passport mailed to you or you could arrange to pick it up at a nearby location from a list that they provide. I didn't want to take the chance of losing the passport in the mail, so I arrange for *Joey* to accompany *Aileen* for the pickup.

The Long Awaited Trip To The U.S.

Aileen's interview was on January 6, 2017 but her visa wasn't ready till around March 20. So you can imagine the anticipation. And would you believe during this time, we got into more arguments? I don't remember exactly why but it wasn't good because she was asking me to buy a round-trip ticket in case things didn't work out. Aileen was not always polite in her choice of words. At times she would literally use the F*** word or other vulgar language in her text and act like she didn't care if we called the whole thing off. Another thing I noted was that if we argued to the point where we talk about canceling, she would literally tear up papers or clothes and send me pictures of the mess on the floor. Me, I didn't want to pay for a round-trip ticket since a return trip was unpredictable. I also held to the possibility that things would change for the better once she was with me. I thought we were both stressed at how long the process was taking. But I was so worried over that last argument that that night I asked myself whether I SHOULD call the whole thing off. We can suffer an upset now and go our separate ways; but it's a whole other thing for her to come and the situation gets worse. In the latter case, she would have already left family and friends and be a long way from home. But I still wanted to give it a try. I thought maybe, just maybe, things would work out. After all, we'd come this far and it seemed foolish to throw it all away. But after things settled down, we continued to chat and make plans for her trip.

THE ARRIVAL: I wanted her first trip to be special. So I spent an additional $300 to book her a flight on Emirates. Once again, I was lucky to find a one-way flight for about $1,000. I made her reservation for March 28, 2017. I told some family members that *Aileen* was finally coming to the U.S. Unfortunately none were available to accompany me to the airport. I was a bit nervous and remember waiting nearly an hour after her plane landed. Everyone had come off the plane and she still hadn't shown up. It turned out that she was just delayed at immigration. She finally walked out with a new Filipino friend she made on the plane. And there, we saw each other again after all that time apart.

I was happy she was here and we gave each other a kiss on the cheeks with a light smile. I was also anxious about the arguments we've had and wondered if I hadn't just made a major mistake. And remember what I said about *Aileen*'s appearance at the airport in Manila? Seeing her again, a year later, brought back some of that same feeling. Her facial skin condition and smile did not give me much to smile about. But I thought that maybe a different climate and environment could help clear up her *Melasma* and brighten her personality. I also thought in due time, she could see a dentist. I didn't hide the fact that I was not happy with her smile; we had discussed it in the Philippines. She has a very nice closed smile, but a smile where her teeth are exposed could be improved. And by the way, I too needed some dental work; maybe not as much. Anyway, I knew this was not the most important thing. Also I remembered the good times we had, her cute facial expression and personality, that I DO like.

So *Aileen* was now in the U.S! We got over the first and second impression and were ready to build on our relationship. I couldn't wait for us to have dinner together, go out to the movies and enjoy different things. This was a whole new experience for her at the age of 46. She had come half way around the world to be with me. She left behind a 24 year-old son and an 18-year old daughter. She also left behind a brother and three sisters, many friends, her nephew *Willy* and her trusted brother-in law *Joey*. She had become my responsibility now. And in addition to being her soon to be husband, I wanted to make her time here memorable. I also reminded myself we had 90 days to get married. And if for any reason things got out of hand, we'd have to go our separate ways. It was probably not the best thing to be thinking about; but given what had happened between us, I think it would be silly for the thought not to cross anyone's mind.

CHAPTER 2: BITTER CULTURE

A big challenge *Aileen* and I faced had to do with our two very different cultures. It's one thing to learn about one's culture in the heat of courtship, but it's another when it comes to living through them when other stress factors are involved.

Food
I like my native Haitian food and *Aileen* likes her Filipino food. When I first tasted Pinoy rice I thought it was horrible; no salt and no spice. *Aileen* would have to add salt if I was going to eat it. When she came to the U.S., she got used to Haitian rice, pork, chicken and much of our custom food. I've also grown accustomed to **pancit** *(noodles)* and a few other Pinoy dishes. And although *Aileen* enjoyed certain Haitian food, she never seemed predisposed to learning how to cook it. As a compromise, she'd cook fish and vegetables. And to make up for the difference we ate fast-foods like McDonald's, Chinese, Kentucky Fried Chicken, Pollo Tropical, etc.

Religion
I knew from the start that *Aileen* and I differed in our faith. I was born and raised Catholic but along the way became a Protestant. I do Bible studies online and have some strong Christian beliefs. I was never really too sure about her religious background; although I know she believes in God and tries to live accordingly. I also know that you can never find the perfect Christian mate. But *Aileen*, at least believed; and I thought as long as we had mutual respect along this line, we could get along. At times, we might hold different views on some things but not enough, I think to cause separation.

Morality
Although this has to do with religion, It may also tie into Filipino values. From what I understand, The Philippines is the only country in the world where ending a marriage is not just difficult, but against the law. The only option for most citizens is to get an annulment, which is long and expensive. As mentioned before, when I went to visit *Aileen*, she suggested that we marry there to save time. Of course, I

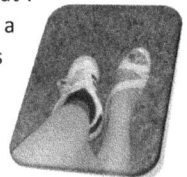

said NO. She didn't make a big deal of it at the time, except sometime in March 2017; she was frustrated with all the chat logs the Embassy was asking for and began to blame it on me for not having married her then.

Aileen has very strong moral values. In her eyes she was more righteous than all other Filipinas. When we talked about how some of my friends would raise the question of Filipino women being mostly interested in getting a visa and green card, she'd not only get upset but also point out that while many are, it wasn't true with her. So determining your fiancé's true motive on this front can be a real problem.

Family values are also things that might come up. When I'd talk about how most of my brothers and sisters were divorced, *Aileen* would throw it right back at me in arguments. Accusing my culture of being crazy and selfish for not being able to stay married.

When I was in the Philippines we went to visit a friend of hers in Biñan. When we were leaving, I was saying goodbye and leaned over to give the friend a kiss on the cheek. She sort of pulled back, thinking that maybe I was coming on to her. *Aileen* went nuts, wondering what was I thinking. I explained that it's customary in the U.S. But the more I tried to explain, the more upset she got thinking I had a personal interest in her friend. We went home that night without speaking to each other. I suggested she call her friend and explain the misunderstanding. She said she would but I'm not sure if she ever did.

I also mentioned previously that *Aileen* did not always have respectful words when we disagreed on things: Often using words like "F***, Punyeta, black guy, negro…" Once she was upset about something and began to make noise by throwing plastic hangers and another object on the floor in our condo. When I confronted her, she would say that it's her way of getting my attention. This was later echoed by the administrator of her 90-Day Fiancé group on Facebook. More on that later.

I find it interesting that on a couple of occasions we'd get separated at the mall or a flea market. Then I'd answer a call on my phone and wander away for a few minutes. She looks all over for me and finds my phone busy when she'd try to call. Coming back, she'd tell me how she thought I had left her. I'm not sure if this is part of the Filipino culture or whether she felt that her actions caused me to literally abandon her in this country. It could be guilt on her part, but it again showed how insecure she can be.

Language Barrier

Although *Aileen* speaks and understands English, this is still a cultural difference to take seriously. There are times when I think she understands what I'm saying, and it turns out I have to repeat myself or explain further. Likewise she would say things where I find myself asking her to repeat what she says. And when that happens too often she gets upset and raises her voice as if to say "why do I need to repeat myself?" When we watched movies, I've had to explain quite a bit for her to keep up. I didn't mind it, of course. I thought to myself that as time went by, she would eventually learn more. But that's something that could take many years depending on the person's intellect. *Aileen*'s native language is Tagalog and she has a very sexy voice when she speaks it. I think Tagalog can be romantic; at times I'd ask her to speak to me in it for practice. Maybe I could learn it faster than she could learn English, which would give us another way of communicating.

The lesson here is that when you date or marry someone whose native tongue is not your own, you may face some challenges. You may not laugh at the same jokes or may respond to situations differently. But if you and your partner are on the same language level, it makes communication easier. Too many misunderstandings, I think, could lead to separation or divorce.

CHAPTER 3: BITTER JEALOUSY

Previously I talked about *Aileen* 's anger and jealousy. I got a glimpse of it before and during my stay in the Philippines. However, it didn't really resonate until she came to the U.S. Shortly after her arrival we got into an argument one night where she was already packing her bags and wanting to leave. Or maybe pretending to want to leave, since that seems to be her way of getting someone's attention. I don't remember the reason behind the argument, but we were on the verge of having more of them!

Invasion Of Privacy

I did unfriend the three Filipino women I had been chatting with before and during my friendship with *Aileen*. But I found out later that she'd also blocked them from my Facebook account. One of them is *Sophie*; and in an effort to let her know that there were no ill feelings, I waved to her on messenger. She later waved back. Shortly after, Aileen was going through my messages, and saw that. That night became a nightmare and showed me a side of *Aileen* I had never seen before. She began cursing, hitting and kicking me HARD, smacking me in the face, throwing things at me and saying "punyeta ka!" asking why I unblocked them after she had blocked them! She called that being unfaithful and said I had no respect for her. She even hocked her throat to spit in my face. She did that on one other occasion also. I'm not a violent person; so I could only play defense by holding her arms to avoid her blows. When I did, her wrists became red and she tried to bite my hands.

Another incident occurred with *Marlene*; one of the other Filipino friends I chatted with before her. Somehow *Aileen* saw us flirting together with her sending me a picture in her underwear. *Marlene* and I had become good friends to the point that we had talked about me visiting her in Manila. She knew one of my sisters from our chats and would often ask me to say *hi*.

In the Philippines, *Aileen* said she had asked me if I had a girlfriend and that I lied when I said NO. First of all, I don't even remember her asking me that and second, just like I was getting to know *Aileen*, *Marlene* and I were just friends. So I didn't feel obligated to tell *Aileen* about any sensitive talk between us. And as I tried to explain and mentioned *Marlene*'s name, Aileen just flipped and started to hit me over the head saying "STOP SAYING HER NAME!!!" At this point she began to mention all my "GIRLFRIENDS" including my ex-wife, and another girl I had dated for six months. She went through my photo albums and destroyed pictures of these women including those other family members of mine had been in. One time she smacked me so hard when I wasn't looking and almost took out my left eye. She was using my cell phone to search for more conversations. As I tried to take it away from her, she threatened to smash it with a hammer. All this was around 2 o'clock in the morning. She was slamming doors on the second floor of the condo where we stayed. I told her to calm down so as not to disturb the people downstairs. I even threatened to call the Police. And being undocumented, things could get complicated and she could be sent home. But she kept saying "I don't care!"

In addition, *Aileen* got on my Facebook account and began to send nasty messages to *Marlene* and *Sophie* in Tagalog. The language included profanity and the F*** Word. She accused *Marlene* of preying on guys like me by pretending she needed money for a surgery for something *Aileen* said does not cost as much. I never sent any money to *Marlene* for any surgery, but *Aileen* wasted no time to accuse her of exaggerating in order to get money from me. She also had numerous exchanges with *Sophie* after taking over my computer. I tried to send messages to *Sophie* from my cell phone asking her to ignore *Aileen*. *Marlene* also sent me messages threatening to take legal action against *Aileen* if she didn't stop stalking her. *Aileen* eventually calmed down later that night and expressed some level of remorse. In the morning, she helped me go through those accounts and delete all those bad messages.

Ex-Girlfriend
On one or two other occasions, *Aileen* would keep me up half the night by playing loud music; purposely turning up the TV volume after another argument. She would bring up my ex-girlfriend *Mimosa* and text me pictures of her or other sexy pictures of women she pulled off the internet. My ex-girlfriend had more boobs and booty than *Aileen* and she'd often accuse me of still being in love with her because I like big booty, she says. She would say things like, "Go fuck them!" by bringing the phone to my face, in anger, to show me pictures.

We talked about not being right for each other and that maybe we should move on to finding our soulmates. When there's love there's more exciting intimacy like sex in the shower, more kissing etc. Although things had not worked out between *Mimosa* and I, I made the mistake of mentioning that we'd had sex in the shower. So when we fought, *Aileen* would accuse me of loving *Mimosa* more because of that. At least not to the same extent; there's been one or two occasions when we did fool around in the shower. But *Aileen* also blamed me for my divorce and any past relationships that she knows of; saying it's my fault I ended up alone; that no one could trust me because I am unfaithful.

Death Threat
Once *Aileen* and I went to a Laundromat and while waiting for the clothes, we began to talk about the action of a brother-in-law of mine who had a child with another woman where his wife later found out. They were on the brink of separation which caused commotion in the family. I had mentioned it to *Aileen* before she came to the U.S. and she said that if I ever did that to her, she would kill me! We somehow came back on that topic and her feelings were just as strong. As mentioned before, *Aileen* had gotten her police clearances in Manila. And other than the anger she demonstrated when she talked with her sister in Canada, I had no reason to believe she has killer instinct. In the Philippines, she seemed to have a very good relationship with her family and friends. But either way, I didn't take that threat lightly.

Chad's Girlfriend
My best friend from High School, *Chad* lives close by and had a girlfriend visiting from Columbia. A few times, all four of us would go to the beach, hang out in downtown Miami or at the park. His girlfriend, I think was younger than *Aileen* with a very sexy body. She liked to wear clothes some would consider provocative. And even though I never gave *Aileen* reasons to think that I had any interest in her, she

would sometimes accuse me of liking her body. But that didn't surprise me since *Aileen* often accuses our culture of being too liberal. And although they became friends and we'd go out, *Aileen* thought she was a show off and kept her at a certain distance. In this case, I happened to share those sentiments; it's among the reasons, I liked *Aileen* in the first place.

Othello Syndrome

As we got into more of the same arguments, I ask myself if there was a reason behind *Aileen's* extreme jealousy. She continued to blame me of unfaithfulness and believes that her actions are justified. One morning I Googled *Jealousy* and came across what's known as **Othello Syndrome** or **Morbid Jealousy**. *Wikipedia* defines it this way:

> *Pathological jealousy, also known as Morbid jealousy,*
> *Othello syndrome or delusional jealousy, is a psychological*
> *disorder in which a person is preoccupied with the thought that*
> *their spouse or sexual partner is being unfaithful without having*
> *any real proof, along with socially unacceptable or abnormal behavior*

I looked up the related symptoms and found the following, among others:

- Feeling jealous
- Being anxious
- Low self-esteem.
- Accusing partner of looking or giving attention to other people
- Not allowing any social media accounts, Facebook, Twitter etc
- Going through the partner's belongings
- Always asking where the partner is and who they're with
- Isolating partner from their family and friends
- Controlling the partner's social circle
- Verbal and/or physical violence towards the partner
- Blaming the partner and establishing an excuse for jealous behavior
- Denying the jealous behavior
- Threatening to harm others or themselves.

I was shocked at the similarities of these symptoms to what I was experiencing. It all seemed to make sense. So out of love, I tried to explain it to *Aileen*. I saw her as someone who was crying out for help but didn't know how to express it. But she kind of chuckled, and dismissed it. She was convinced I was the problem. She said to me "You think I'm crazy?" SHE accuses ME of being crazy, bipolar and anxious. I thought that if she was suffering from a mental disorder, I don't think I could change that. I'm not a psychiatrist and trying to get help for it might only complicate things.

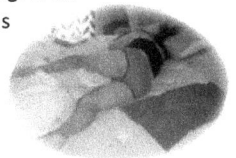

After a while I had to be careful about what I said to *Aileen* or shared with her. Once, in an intimate chat I took some naked pictures of myself to show her. Sometime later, in an argument, she threatened to share those same pictures with my women friends, ex-girlfriend even my ex-wife! In the end, she never did. Maybe it's because I told her I'd never talk to her again if that happened. *Aileen* sometimes uses extremely colorful language when she talks; below is a small sample of our chat messages:

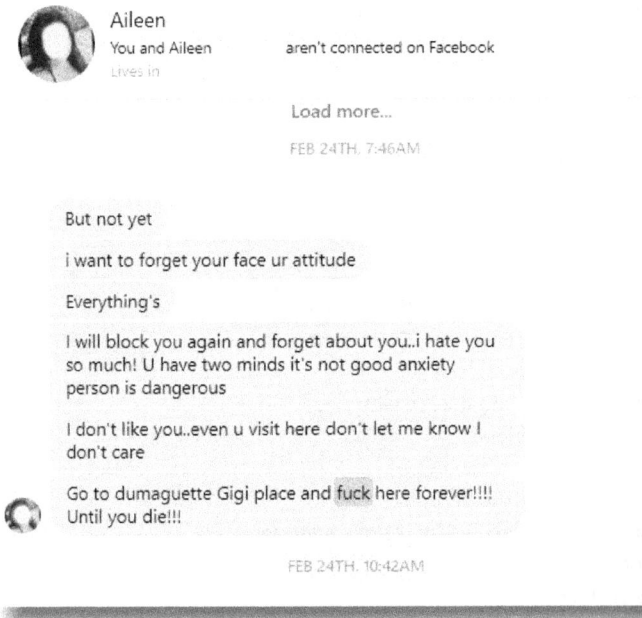

Aileen
You and Aileen   aren't connected on Facebook
Lives in

Load more...

FEB 24TH, 7:46AM

But not yet

i want to forget your face ur attitude

Everything's

I will block you again and forget about you..i hate you so much! U have two minds it's not good anxiety person is dangerous

I don't like you..even u visit here don't let me know I don't care

Go to dumaguette Gigi place and fuck here forever!!!! Until you die!!!

FEB 24TH, 10:42AM

Load more...

FEB 24TH. 1:22AM

Reject!

Again and again and again!

Its better one of us will die! To forget anything!

I cant accept tht u play my emotion!

Because of ur anxiety

Anxiety abd bipolar!

And not trust

Pre nup

And insult my children

My family

again?

SAT 9:07PM

I send u photos

Fuck her again

I know u like to go out to find a fucking girl

Coz u r easy guy

Friendly guy

Fuck u Dante's

Don't say u push me back here..no!! Coz u r money face

Moneyyface

U want me for work

And take money

That's righty

Load more...

Or u find out on fb

Lots of women on fb make them gf and masturbate them

To complete ur pleasure

Oh u wanna go back To mimose good

I know u hate her u said but I saw ur message to her that u love her more

That's wht u said fuck you!

I never feel that from you

U ignore my y feelings!

Even appearance like that I'm blind

Black guyy

Panget

Don't wish

u are the one

Wish urself

U imagine things

Dickey!

Punyeta ka

Punyeta k

Evil

U just proving i was right

Evil

Evil

Fight

It's not good

We just dnt have much in common

So its ok

I wish u the best po

Prenup that's not good.. If u marry again for pilipina don't do that she will hate you

That's my advice

Even we r poor I can't do that

Bye Dante's thank you u feed me there

Ty...

Load more...

CHAPTER 4: BITTER INFLUENCE

If you ever decide to take 90-Day challenge, think about the people who may impact your decisions. You'll get a variety of advice, but in the end you'll have to follow your own heart. I'll talk a little about *Aileen*'s family and friends, but will mostly outline the impact mines had on us.

Best Friend

Chad is my best friend in Florida. We went to high school together and had not seen each other for twenty years. Now he lives about ten minutes away from me. He is retired from the Navy and has traveled around the world, including the Philippines. He had much to offer on what he thought was the goal of Filipino women searching for love online. When I told him about my desire to go to the Philippines to begin a 90-Day fiancé with *Aileen*, he sent me the following text:

Man don't know why you're going to PI? God has nothing to do with it! You should have talked to me first! I have been to the PI at least 12 times. Sometimes for as long as Month or so. Why do you supposed I didn't marry a Filipina? If you're going to party/pleasure that's a candy store. You cannot trust these women. They will love you no shit/ treat you like a king until she gets her freaking Green Card! And your ass is SOL And don't tell me this one is different?? I have also lived in Hawaii and California. You should see how those wives/Women behave. I have also dated supposedly wives in California. Do you know how many relatives she has All over California/New York waiting for some Sucker to bring her over? And also relatives waiting to bring over once she settled. This is not your seen or play ground My Brother. It's a great place to party/Play but not look for a wife!!! 9 Out Of 10 are no good (Bastos), waiting for a foreign Sucker (European/Arabs/But preferably American).   Not your seen Bro. Sinners Land. Sincerely/Regretfully, Your Brother, Chad.

Aileen knew that *Chad* was my best friend and that I share some things with him. I remember mentioning his feelings towards Filipinas. Needless to say, *Aileen* was not his biggest fan. And no matter how I tried to convince her that *Chad*'s experience may not be my own, she would blame him when we argue. But still, we'd go out together with *Chad* and his girlfriend from time to time.

As mentioned, *Chad*'s girlfriend was kind of flashy in the way she dressed. And *Aileen*, being old fashioned, didn't have any problem making it known; usually in the form of ignoring her. What I tell her is that it's OK if you don't like someone, but try not to make it too obvious. *Chad* was nice enough to pick us up in his car to go to the beach or for a night out downtown.

But things got a little heated one day when *Chad* and his girlfriend suggested we all go out to a movie. Due to an argument we had earlier, *Aileen* said she didn't want to go. While I was trying to convince her, *Chad* called. And as I was telling him that *Aileen* was thinking about not going, she tried to forcefully take the phone away from me. In her anger, she also threw some water on me. In fact just prior to that she had dipped a towel in the toilet and threaten to hit me with it. That didn't go well with *Chad* when I mentioned it later. I told *Aileen* it was rude to do this with *Chad* hearing everything on the phone. But as usual, she said "I don't care!" Later she did calm down and we ended up going out anyway.

My Sisters

My older sister, **Ate** *Nelia*, a registered nurse, was closest to *Aileen*. **Ate** is Tagalog for **Sister**; particularly to show respect to an older Sister. They were already friends on Facebook even before *Aileen* came to the U.S. She knew about *Aileen*'s jealousy and often told her that it's devilish.

Aileen liked *Ate Nelia* very much and was more comfortable around her. Sometimes *Nelia* would pick her up to spend a day or two at her house. Once, she cooked Pancit *(noodles)* for *Ate Nelia*. Almost once a week, *Aileen* and I would visit her to watch a DVD movie and order Chinese food. Other times we'd go out to eat at a Filipino restaurant close to *Ate Nelia*'s house. She also had a massage chair that *Aileen* liked spending time in. *Aileen* also loved *Ate Nelia's* dog, *Mercedes*. But since they were friends, my sister would always know when there was friction between us. And when *Aileen* put on the show of tearing up my pictures, hitting me, spitting on me, *Nelia* was shocked and didn't think we should get married. She said *Aileen* seems so sweet. But when *Aileen* talked to her about us, she never tells her the whole story. Anyway, despite our differences, *Ate Nelia* still likes *Aileen*. She would simply follow my lead and be OK with whatever decision I made.

My eldest sister, **At** *Evelyne* is a retired, registered nurse. She, on the other hand, was not so nice towards *Aileen*. At first she was looking forward to meeting her and was happy that I had found what could be the right person. Especially after my prior six-month relationship. My sister is close to me and I do value her opinion. But after I told her about the fights *Aileen* and I had, Her first response was "SHE IS SICK!" *Evelyne* also is speaking from experience; one that reminded her of the dark days she went through in her marriage when she was the victim of mental and physical abuse. She thought that Aileen was abusive. And after detailing *Aileen*'s actions, she said most men would put her on a plane and send her back home A.S.A.P! She strongly urged me against the marriage and thought I should thank God for revealing that side of *Aileen* before we tie the knot. That said, *Evelyne* never got to meet *Aileen*.

Ate Kettly is also a retired, registered nurse. She is between the ages of *Ate Evelyne* and *Ate Nelia*. She had recently moved to Florida from New York. I wasn't as close to her when it comes to openly sharing my relationships. *Aileen*'s behavior, at first, caught me by surprise and I felt the need to talk to those closest to me. We sometimes visited *Kettly*. But, unlike *Ate Nelia*, *Aileen* was always shy and had very little to say. She would hold on to me and smile whenever *Ate Kettly* asked her how things were going.

The language barrier was also a factor. Either way, it was going to take some time before *Aileen* could bond with other members of my family.

Daran And Erick

These two are my sons; both in their late 20s. Before *Aileen* came to the U.S., *Erick* asked me whether I was sure she was not mainly interested in a green card. Of course, I tried to convince him otherwise. Those two were never too close to *Aileen*. They met her and seen her a couple of times when we visited them. One time she was very helpful in helping me and the boys move some furniture and equipment from their garage. *Daran* is a tattoo artist. Even though *Aileen* doesn't like tattoos, she was always open to the possibility of getting a small butterfly on her right shoulder from him. But somehow we never got around to it. *Erick* once asked me if *Aileen* spoke any English. Because she's not fluent in it, she was often shy. This limited her ability to fully interact with the boys.

Julie

I didn't really have any close interaction with *Aileen*'s younger sister *Julie* from Canada. We spoke on the phone for about thirty minutes when I was in the Philippines. She told me how *Aileen* has a good heart and worked for a long time in the *UAE*, for very little pay. She said *Aileen* would always be thinking about her family: sending them money, boxes of canned goods and other essentials. But she'd always complain how she never got anything in return from certain members of her family. Understandably, *Julie* was concerned about her sister possibly getting hurt in this process. Since I didn't have much to go on at the time, I could only reassure *Julie* that my intentions were honorable; and that regardless of the outcome, I would do my best to protect her sister.

When *Aileen* and I began having issues in the U.S., I was considering calling off the wedding. *Aileen* of course is usually on her phone updating family and friends of our situation. And the main thing they told her was that if I was having second thoughts about the wedding, I never truly loved her. *Julie* suggested she go back home and not try to force me into marriage. I never discussed our problems with *Julie*, nor did she ever ask to talk to me.

Aileen's Son And Daughter

Aileen had a son and a daughter from the guy she was with in the Philippines. I said *hi* to her son over video but never talked to him beyond that. Her daughter *Joy* was the one I included as a K-2 recipient. I thought if things worked out with *Aileen*, we would follow up on it. *Joy* was very close to her mom. They text each other almost daily. But when things began to break down between me and *Aileen*, *Joy* encouraged her mom to return home due to the stress she was under. In an earlier version of a prenup I stated that I would not be liable for her children because they were adults. This was a mistake on my part. I was trying to save money by doing this on my own. With my background I know enough, I thought, to at least research these legal matters. Some prenup forms are free online so I went ahead and drafted the first version.

Later I realized there was no need to mention the kids at all if they are adults. So I revised the prenup with a much cleaner one. I drafted it even though I was undecided about the wedding. I thought as the

90 days close in, I should at least take care of the things we would need if we went ahead with the marriage. *Aileen* shared the first version of the prenup with *Joy*. I told her she should not have done that. Why put her daughter in that position, knowing how much she cares about her? So in addition to *Joy* asking her to come back to the Philippines, Aileen was also busy accusing me of insulting her and her family with the prenup.

Aileen's Facebook Group

This was a 90-Day Fiancé group designed to give advice and support to those going through the process. As far as I know, the group seemed to be made mostly of Filipinos. *Aileen* had called the admin of the group to try and persuade me to marry. When I told her about *Aileen*'s behavior, she thought that *Aileen* was "trying to get my attention!" Hmmm, now where have I heard that before? *Aileen* has said the same thing in trying to justify her behavior. I thought this must be common among Filipinos. But if this is her way of getting my attention, she was sadly mistaken! All that does is add to my frustration and destroys any chances we have of moving forward.

And when *Aileen* shared the prenup with other members of her group, one of them told her that this should be the least of her worries. She advised *Aileen* to sign it. She explained that after she gets her green card, she would be free to petition other members of her family. I saw that text looking into *Aileen*'s phone after she left it unattended nearby. When I asked her about that advice, she said she didn't take it seriously because that's not her style. Somehow I believed that and gave her credit for it. Otherwise, she would not have resisted in the first place, right? And later on, she did soften up and agreed to sign the prenup. One thing that aggravated me was her constantly telling me how other members of her group were happy in their 90-Day experience. I told her I didn't care about what others are doing and neither should she. It's best to focus on OUR problems and ways to try and solve them.

Ayan's Advice

Being troubled with the uncertainties, I began to search for answers online. I came across a blog where a woman name **Ayan** had happily gone through this visa process as the fiancée of a U.S. petitioner. I sent her an email and explained the problems *Aileen* and I were having. I also asked her about ways *Aileen* could stay in the U.S. legally without me having to change her status. Also if it were possible for someone else to sponsor *Aileen* if we got married and later divorced. But the obvious answer was that I, the petitioner, have to sign the affidavit of support *(I-864)*. A co-sponsor can also sign, but only to supplement the petitioner's income if necessary.

Ayan's feedback was that the affidavit of support is not to be taken lightly. She said she knew of women who've used it in a vindictive manner to get back at their spouses. The responsibility goes beyond someone applying for public assistance if they can't find a job. Disgruntled spouses have purposely chosen not to work and sue their petitioner husband or wife for the financial support. In other words, once you sign the affidavit of support you are legally obligated for the financial well-being of your spouse until he or she completes 40 quarters of work *(usually 10 years)* or until they become a U.S. citizen. And if this is ever taken to court, a judge will rule in favor of that spouse.

For this reason, she thought that if things were not working out, it would be best for *Aileen* to return home and try to find some other way of coming back to the U.S. As I said before, I don't mind getting advice from others, but the final decision has to come from me. Sadly I thought *Ayan* had a good point and confirmed what was already on my mind.

CHAPTER 5: THE WEDDING

The 90-Day clock was ticking! And the closer we got to June 28, 2017 the more stress we were under. I wanted *Aileen* to stay. But under the circumstances, I had a hard time sleeping at night. Her family and friends seemed against the marriage. They thought if I didn't want to get married, it's because I never loved her. But I don't think *Aileen* was telling them the things she did that was causing me to have doubts. My sister *Evelyne* and best friend *Chad*, were telling me that *Aileen*'s morbid jealousy is cultural in nature and would never change.

To Marry Or Not To Marry?

I was so troubled by this that I tried to make reservations for *Aileen* to return home. If she went over the 90 days, she would begin to accrue unlawful presence in the U.S. From my understanding, if you overstay for less than six months *(180 days)*, you can still be granted another visa or green card. But you're considered to be **Tago Ng Tago** *(TNT)* *"Filipino for illegal alien in hiding."* But even though I proposed that she at least stay for the six-month grace period, *Aileen* was afraid of being TNT; she kept saying **Mag TNT ako? Hinde!** *(Me TNT? No way!)* She'd rather go back home. At least she seemed honest on that front. She reminded me that if we didn't get married we will have wasted all the time, money and energy we invested. She would lose legal status and have to start all over again.

The other option was a quick civil wedding that would allow her to legally stay without a real time limit to adjust status. I've read stories where others adjust status after one or two years. The *USCIS* encourages you to adjust status as soon as possible after the wedding. The good news is *Aileen* would not be TNT, which would lift tremendous pressure off of us.

No Ring, No Dress

Aileen would accuse me of not loving her because I hadn't committed to buying her a ring or wedding dress; or even officially proposed for that matter. It's funny, but *USCIS* will tell you that the 90-Day visa is NOT to see whether or not you are compatible. You should have already determined that and made the related plans to marry your fiancé. But, for me, the problem is the time spent with *Aileen* in the Philippines was not enough for either of us to really decide. And I don't consider chatting online for one year a good way of getting to know someone.

Having said that, I was reluctant to buying a ring and dress for two reasons: (1) I couldn't afford it without sacrificing a good chunk of my savings and (2) I began to have doubts after *Aileen* came to the U.S. As for the proposal, given the circumstances, I thought I'd take things one day at a time. But I did have a backup plan: to use any rings we had available and get a non-traditional wedding. And depending on how things went from there, we would formalize the wedding two years down the road; which is the time period given with the provisional green card.

Prenuptial Agreement

I talked earlier about the events surrounding the prenup I had proposed to *Aileen*. I also mentioned that she wasn't happy with it. She felt offended and didn't hesitate to use nasty words to express her anger. We had only known each other for a short time and I thought it would be wise to protect our individual assets; especially mines. I drafted the prenup myself because I didn't want to spent close to the $1,500 the attorneys were asking. By the way, I saved money overall in the process by filing all the immigration forms we needed, myself.

Aileen felt insulted and sad when she compared my assets to hers. She tells me to EAT my prenup if I thought she was interested in my properties. I don't have a problem with her being upset. But I did have an issue with how she assumed I should just trust her. Wouldn't it have been easier if she agreed to the prenup to prove good intentions? Either way, her friends had finally convinced her to sign it.

About a month before the 90-day deadline, I got *Chad* and my sister *Kettly* to be witnesses to the prenup at a local notary. I drafted it because I wanted us to be ready in case I decided to go forward with the wedding. I then put the papers away and continued to work on our differences.

Marriage License

Around mid June, 2017 I thought about getting the marriage license. That would give us three days to decide whether or not to go through with it. Just like the prenup, I wanted to get that out of he way. I was feeling sorry for *Aileen* and thinking how devastating it would be if she had to go back. I brought up the three-day time frame for the license and she agreed we should get it. That cost about $100 and would give us that extra time to decide. So on Monday June 19, we went to the courthouse, filed the application and paid the fee. The license could be used on or after June 22 and would expire on August 20th of the same year.

Aileen's I-94 *(arrival record on passport)* expired on June 28. At the courthouse I was telling her that if all went well, she could become a citizen in three years. We met another couple there who had come seeking a divorce because things were not working out for them; like we really needed to hear that right now! I was also going through my phone and showed *Aileen* some pictures I took of the photos she had ripped up one night that littered the living room floor. With a cheerful face, she said to me "delete that! because it would not happen again."

First Attempt

When the three days expired on June 22, I was still undecided. *Aileen* thought we would not be getting married. On Friday June 23, I told her to get dressed but didn't say where we were going. I was planning on going to the courthouse to get married so I made sure she had a ring *Ate Nelia* gave her. I pretended we were just driving around and stopped at a nearby McDonald's two blocks away from the courthouse. We ate and talked for a while. The marriage division was closing at 3:30. We left McDonald's around 1 and continued driving around. I wasn't sure if *Aileen* had remembered the area. I drove past the courthouse still trying to decide on going in. But as I drove away, she asked me why we went past the courthouse? That took me by surprise and I said "you remembered?" She said "of course!" My heart was pounding as I turned around to go back. We parked for a few minutes and talked again about whether we should do this. Obviously nothing I said at this point would matter. *Aileen* was here to get married, period!

We left the nearby parking, and got closer to the courthouse. I saw a well groomed man passing by and stopped him. He came and stood by the passenger window where *Aileen* was sitting. I kindly asked if he would give us some feedback on a difficult decision. I explained *Aileen* is from the Philippines, blah blah blah, and that we were planning to go to the courthouse to get married. However, we've had some real issues and I was still undecided. He told us that if we're having problems now, we should seriously reconsider because marriage is a BIG step. Of course, I knew that, but I guess I wanted *Aileen* to hear it from someone else. So I thanked him and began to drive away. When I turned and looked at *Aileen*, the expression on her face was almost indescribable. She looked at me like a kid whose candy I just stole! She started panting heavily and her eyes began to tear up. I tried to stay strong as I drove away. A few blocks down the road, *Aileen* lost it! She threw left-over coffee from McDonald's on me as well as water from a bottle we had in the car. She started screaming and even tried to take the wheel away from me and steer the car into oncoming traffic. I know she was hurt, but I blame myself. I should not have teased her and driven past the courthouse if I wasn't ready to go through with it. Maybe I did because somewhere inside I wanted to do it. I thought about what would happen if we didn't get married. So it was either we go through the heartbreak now and avoid bigger problems later on, or get married and end the 90-Day nightmare.

Plea For Forgiveness

Aileen was **kawawa** *(Tagalog for a wretch)*. When she cries, it's hard for me not to be emotional. Sometimes when I wake up in the morning I hear her weeping either in the living room or the bathroom. And of course, I would always to try to console her. One time, I caught her with a big knife she'd taken from the kitchen and seemed to be wanting to cut herself. But something told me she was just "trying to get my attention!" It didn't look like she really wanted to hurt herself.

In the final days, I was still very nervous and thought it would be best not to marry under the circumstances. All this was shortly after she had a birthday. I booked her a flight late Monday that was to leave on Tuesday June 27; the day before her visa expired. I'd made several reservations in the past, but for one reason or another we couldn't get past the emotion and I've had to cancel each one. Good thing, I was making them through **Priceline.com.** They give you 24 hours to cancel for a full refund. That day, I had until 11 p.m. to cancel.

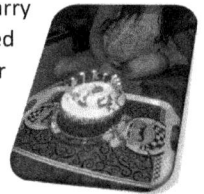

And at times, with each reservation, *Aileen* would let her folks know she was coming back. And she's also had to tell *Joey* to get ready to pick her up at the airport. So you can imagine how some of the pressure was also being felt by her family and friends back home.

To remind myself why we were not getting married, I made a list of the things *Aileen* had done that got me so concerned. I called it *Why I had to let Aileen go* and wrote the following on a piece of paper:

- Kicked me hard repeatedly
- Spit in my face, twice
- Slapped me
- Destroyed my albums
- Pushed torn pictures up my face
- Pulled my hair, bit me, pinched me, leaving scars
- Cursed and called me **"negro"**
- Blocked my friends on Facebook
- Cursed - dirty language, messaging friends with my Facebook profile
- Soaked towel in toilet to hit me
- Called me **"fucking man"**
- Asked me to stick my penis in a bottle and watch dirty YouTube videos
- Falsely accused me of having sex with others.

The night before, she was hugging me and asking for forgiveness with tears in her eyes. She looks up at me with puppy-like eyes promising to change and do better. She kept saying "Mahal, Mahal, I'm sorry! We've always said *despite our trials... Mahal forgive me."* This was not the first time she'd apologized. But this time it touched my heart more than ever. I knew marriage would be a big step for us and I didn't have any guarantee things would be different.

The following day on the 27, *Aileen* kept sobbing, crying on the sofa. I barely slept, thinking about what would happen that day. I stayed in the bedroom trying not to run into her. Her flight was scheduled for 7 p.m. Around noon, I walked passed the living room and saw her weeping. Her eyes were red looking like she'd been crying all night. I decided to share with her what I wrote down. As I read the note she continued sobbing and looked at me and said "Sorry again *po*. Sorry for every**TING**!" I imagined what things will be like once she leaves. I know I'd feel empty inside and it would take some time to heal.

My sister *Evelyne* called me that morning to see how I was doing. When I told her how broken I was and how *Aileen* was in tears, she said that *Aileen* would be fine! She thought this was a form of manipulation on her part. She said I should be strong and reminded me that sometimes it's better to be alone than with the wrong company. Many of my family members are divorced. My friend *Chad* also told me in a text that I did nothing wrong. He said the 90 days, in part, was to see if we are compatible. But he wished me well with whatever decision I made; saying that God would not allow more hardship on me than I could handle.

Back To The Courthouse
Shortly after 12 noon, I was pacing back and forth asking *Aileen* not to make things harder for me than they already were. At the same time I was thinking about the times when we weren't fighting and the

intimate moments. I thought about how marriage would give us the freedom to have more of that intimacy. Yea, I know what you're thinking: SEX can really do that to you! at a critical moment like that, I blotted out the negative and was focusing on cuddling in bed?

I said to *Aileen* "Let's go get married!" asking her to hurry as I looked at the clock. I was happy to see, right then and there, how her face turned from sadness into a smile☐. But as I was driving to the courthouse, I got cold feet again. I said "I can't do it!". *Aileen* said "again?" with a perplexed look. But I kept on driving knowing that the clock was ticking. I thought about turning around, but I've done that before. Only now, we'd run out of time. It was about 1 p.m. when we got to the courthouse. Lucky for us there was only a handful of people. We showed the marriage license and they asked us a few questions. Suddenly an issue came up. My drivers license didn't have *JR* in my name, but I had put it on the marriage license. And in order to avoid problems down the road, we had to make some changes that would delay this process. Then I remembered my passport has *JR* in it. Trouble is, I left it home. I decided to quickly drive there to pick it up. I figured we still had some time since the round trip would take about an hour.

I asked *Aileen* to wait for me in order to save time. This would allow me to jog or run if I had to. But she was worried that I might change my mind again and not come back. You know what? Even though I wasn't planning that, the fact that she brought it up got me thinking on the way home. But this time it was getting more difficult to call it off; I would need an alibi. So I thought to myself, I'll just tell her I couldn't find the passport. Then we'd go past the deadline, making it look like an accident. So when I got home, I put the passport inside my left sock.

Back at the courthouse, *Aileen* was anxiously waiting. I put a worried look on my face as I asked her if she had misplaced my passport. She gave me the same face she did after I had gotten that advice from the guy by courthouse. She was panting hard with a bewildering look. She said she doesn't know anything about my passport! She then said let's go back to the office and explain. I reminded her that the lady said we'd have to make changes to the paperwork and we didn't have time. So with *Aileen* on the verge of tears again and terribly upset, I told her we should go home and get her bags ready for her flight. She said to me "did you plan this?" I tried to keep a straight face. And as we were both walking fast trying to find the exit, I said "What, you don't believe me?" I was so focused on how broken she was and couldn't concentrate on finding the exit. At the same time, I'm thinking whether I should tell her the truth. In other words even at the last minute, my conscience was bothering me. I still thought she deserved a chance. I thought I would later regret it, if I allowed her to go back to the Philippines like this.

We stopped near a staircase close to the exit. I took a deep breath and said to her "you're right, *po*. I did

plan it." I reached into my sock and took the passport out. I can't begin to describe the transformation in her face! She was so happy she managed to crack a smile. Sometimes I have a hard time making decisions in my life, but this was probably the worst. She had every right to be angry but she wasn't. And although I thought I might live to regret this, I just tried to enjoy the moment. We went back to the marriage division, I gave them my passport and they finished the paperwork. **We waited for about fifteen minutes and they called us into the chapel where we took our vows and exchanged rings.** *Aileen* had on a blue and white dress on and I was in jeans and a gray T-shirt. The court clerk who performed the ceremony borrowed my cell phone and snap a few pictures for us.

On the way back home, we came on the topic of marriage laws in the U.S. And *Aileen*'s first question to me was *if we got a divorce, what would happen if she contested it*②. This is one of the areas that had me hesitating on marriage in the first place! I knew all of this going in, but concerns over hurting her feelings had obviously clouded my judgment. But we made it through this giant hurdle and could finally breathe a sigh of relief. When we got back, I canceled her flight to the Philippines.

CHAPTER 6: BITTER STRESS

After we got married, we moved on to the challenge of adjusting *Aileen*'s status. There were times when things were OK between us. But the thought of having to deal with her jealousy and attitude had me concerned about the future. I also began to feel the financial pressure of having to support her. Her daughter *Joy*, would occasionally ask her for help with school back home. So once in a while I'd send money to her daughter through Western Union. But part of the reason for coming to the U.S. was for *Aileen* to get her green card and find work.

For a little bit of background, I graduated college with a Bachelor's Degree in accounting. But in the past twenty years, I've also been involved in real estate investing and game design. I hold a real estate license in Florida. But my main source of income comes from three rental properties I own. The fourth one is a condo where *Aileen* and I lived. My other forms of income, occasionally, come from real estate commissions and freelance accounting work. *Aileen*, on the other hand, graduated High School and has vocational experience and training as a caregiver.

Financial Challenge

In addition to the issues we were having, I realized that it may not even be possible to adjust *Aileen*'s status without a co-sponsor. I mentioned before that the first affidavit of support *(I-134)* is not really looked at with the original petition. But when you're ready to adjust status, you have to submit financial information with the more important affidavit *(I-864)*. That's the one where you pledge to be financially responsible for your spouse; a contract for which you can be sued.

At first I didn't realize I'd have to file that second affidavit. After I did some research, I found that in order for me to take care of *Aileen*, my income had to be at least 125% of the Health and Human Services *(HHS)* poverty guideline.

At the time, for a household of two, the annual amount was $20,300. At first I didn't think that would be an issue because I gross more than that. The problem was I'd have to submit my tax returns with the affidavit. And depreciation on my rental properties, which is a non-cash expense, reduced my income substantially. In fact my average adjusted gross income for the past three years came to $4,454. So I was short by $15,846. But I also learned that if I had equity in assets that's at least three times the shortage *(47,538)*,

I could potentially qualify. My equity in real estate came to about $73,000 (48,000 + 25,000). I say "about" because I would also have to justify these with actual appraisals. But as a realtor, I was able to come up with a rough estimate of value. But if I did submit the affidavit, I would still have to show the appraisals. The average appraisal cost is about $450. So I'd be looking at an extra $900 for the two properties.

But there was still another problem: I could only include assets that can be converted into cash within one year AND without causing considerable hardship to my finances. The immigration officer must be convinced that the value of the assets could be reasonably made available to support *Aileen*. That would take away $25,000 from my equity because the last one on the list is the condo where we live. So that would be considered a hardship and would disqualify the affidavit of support. And even though the $48,000 is slightly above the $47,538 it's still an estimate and the thin margin is not worth the risk. Also the rental is my primary source of income; that too could be a hardship if I were to sell it.

I also thought maybe I could try and convince the immigration officer that the only reason my income is lower on my taxes is because of depreciation. But from what I've read online, that would be a long shot; too complicated and they like to keep things simple. I could also report some freelance income in accounting and taxes, but those are sporadic and may not even be enough to cover the shortage. So even though I knew I could ultimately provide for *Aileen*, at least until she is able to work, the chances of having form I-864 accepted were very slim. And the cost of adjusting status is at least $1,500 and is nonrefundable.

I could have tried to find a job, but I'd been self employed for over twenty years and getting back into the accounting field at the age of 55 would not be easy. I could have even gone to work as a security guard which I used to do many years ago. But that too would call for some measures such as getting a state license and related training courses. And none of this was part of the original plan. Not to mention the uncertainty of our marriage that was looming. Here is a summary of what I've just outlined:

ADJUSTMENT OF STATUS ANALYSIS			
2017 Poverty Guideline:			$20,300
Average Income on Taxes	2016	4,313	
	2015	9,415	
	2014	-367	4,454
Shortage			15,846
Minimum Cash value of Assets (3 times shortage)			$47,538
Approximate Equity in Properties:		Miami	0
		Lakeland	0
		North Miami	48,000
		Main Condo	25,000

A Co-Sponsor

If the petitioner *(ME)* is not financially able to support the immigrant *(Aileen)* we might consider a co-sponsor to fill in the gap. The only one who qualified to do so at the time was *Ate Nelia*. She is a full-time registered nurse and makes good money. She was also the closest one in the family to *Aileen*. But there was only one problem: she was aware of the issues we were having. And as a co-sponsor, she would bear the same financial responsibility. As my sister, I had an obligation to disclose all of this to her. And I could tell that she was very reluctant to commit and I couldn't blame her.

K-2 Visa

My Friend *Chad* once told me, that he thought *Aileen*'s primary concern was to bring her family to the U.S. after she gets her papers. Although I question that to some degree, I couldn't help but wonder when she asked me about it one night. She said that I SAID I would send for her daughter *Joy*. I had to remind her that that wasn't a promise. I included *Joy* as a K-2 recipient because it was convenient. The rest would depend on whether or not I had the money and how things were going between us. We also had to consider where her daughter would live if she did come. Our place is a one-bedroom condo. *Aileen* told me that *Joy* would live in California with her grandparents who had expressed interest in taking her in. But, I had never confirmed that and was a bit skeptical.

Isolation

With the issues of changing *Aileen*'s status, it was hard to find something for her to do. She spent a good deal of her time chatting with family and friends back home. I could tell she missed them but she was willing to stay, hoping somehow I'd be able to adjust her status. She hadn't made any real friends in the U.S. We met a Filipino family at the beach once, but they live a few hours further north in Florida. She has a cousin who'd been living in New York for 15 years doing private-duty caregiving. I suggested that she go stay with her and try to find work there. But *Aileen* didn't seem interested and her cousin was talking about charging her rent, even if she's not working.

We spent most of our days at our community pool, the occasional movie, the park, playing board games and visiting *Ate Nelia* once a week. *Aileen* didn't seem interested in making friends either. She spent a lot of time criticizing the American culture. She often complained about my friend *Chad* because of the views he shared about Filipinas.

Divorce Proposal

Despite everything that happened, I desperately wanted to give *Aileen* a chance. Before the wedding, I tried to think of ways we could marry and separate and still allow her to legally stay in the country. So I came up with the following proposal: we would marry and get a divorce after one year. In the meantime, we could open a bank account together and take out a life insurance policy as proof of having been together. We live under the same roof, so we could easily prove our motives to immigration. Since there was never any intent on our part to commit visa fraud, she would then try to adjust her own status after the divorce. Ordinarily, if this happens, suspicion is often raised. But if it can be shown that we intended to live together and have sufficient proof, It should be enough for her to make a case. She would simply explain that the marriage didn't work out.

However, I found out later, that the only way this would work is if I had already signed the affidavit of support. Otherwise she would still need a sponsor to take on the financial responsibility. From what I understand, only the **original petitioner** is allowed to change her status. But, *Aileen* didn't like the idea in the first place. She thought I was just trying to get rid of her. She said she came to be with me and if we weren't going to be together, she'd just go home. While I applaud her for thinking that way, it still didn't solve the problems we were having.

Unemployed

Without adjusting status, *Aileen* can't get a green card. Without a green card she can't legally work. Before we got married, she said we could even delay adjustment of status for a year or two. But her not being able to work, just added to the stress of the both of us staying home. I spent time working on the computer and she would clean, cook, watch TV and text family back home on her cell phone.

She tried applying for a job at a Filipino restaurant where she had made some friends who became aware of her situation. They advised her NOT to return home but never gave her any assurance of a job. That caused a fight between us: she blames me for not giving her time to work at that restaurant. The restaurant was in Pembroke Pines, close to *Ate Nelia*'s house. Even if she could work there undocumented, transportation would be a big problem. The place was about forty minutes away by car and buses would take well over an hour each way. Me driving her to work that far would not be worth it for the pay. And *Aileen* staying at *Ate Nelia*'s house would not have been a good option for a lot of reasons. I was a bit upset that she was making plans with the restaurant owner without consulting with me. She was obviously stressed and yelled at me in the car saying "OK OK, so I go back!" I didn't mind if she could work there. I was the one who printed the business cards she was sharing over there. But the owner didn't seem to have any plans of hiring her at that time anyway.

The possibility of *Aileen* going back home was increasing. We agreed that if we ever got together again in the future, it would be better to live either in New York or California; cities with more Filipinos and jobs. New York was a particular favorite for *Aileen* because she likes the cold weather and would love to see snow for the first time. There, is also massive public transportation, including subways that would allow her to go out on her own. She would also be closer to other family members. In Florida, you can't really go anywhere without a car. *Aileen* would ultimately need one, learn how to drive and a get driver's license. There is public transportation, but the system is not as diverse as it is in New York.

Aileen Cares

Later I thought I could set *Aileen* up with some freelance work in care giving since she has some experience from the Philippines. And If we could find someone in need of basic care like cleaning and running errands, that might work. So I made some business cards and flyers under the name ***Aileen Cares*** and we began sharing them in the neighborhood; starting with our own community. We even visited and talked to a friend who works on the board of our condo association. I put some ads online that *Aileen* was available for babysitting, cleaning and, or care giving. But we got no response.

Aileen Cares was a good idea, but it seemed that she would have a better chance at it back in the Philippines. And if I got her some basic tools, she could possibly make it work. I also thought jobs there would be easier to find, although the pay would be less. *Aileen* began to be excited about the prospect of having her own business in the Philippines. She agreed there was a need for medical care and she could start with taking blood pressure, glucose reading and other gadgets that are more expensive there. She said she knew people in the field that she could potential work with. She also mentioned she would get her daughter and brother-in-law involved in the business.

I told her my business background would be helpful and that I would also work with her. So I started preparing patient forms that she could use for new clients as well as business cards for her to get the word out. Some family members tried to talk her out of it and told her she should stay in the U.S. But the more we talked about the medical equipment that would make an impression back home, the more *Aileen* seemed to be on board. She also asked me to buy her some caregiver uniform, a medical bag and a backpack for work. I even wanted to pay for some medical courses for her to add more credibility to the business. Another reason for the excitement of the business was that if successful, *Aileen* would be self employed with unlimited income potential. She would feel good about herself and working together could potentially bring us closer and pave the way for a better life in the U.S. I even promised to visit her from time to time to help. Below is part of the start-up cost for *Aileen Cares*:

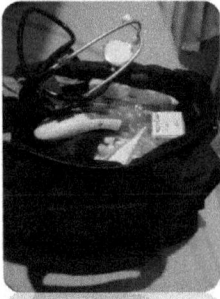

Date	Store	Equipment	Cost
7/21/17	Vista Print	Business Cards	$44
8/16/17	PCMS	Medical Bag	29
7/27/17	PCMS	Pulse Oximeter	44
7/27/17	PCMS	Touchless Forehead Thermostat	52
7/27/17	PCMS	Blood Pressure Machine	48
8/15/17	Ross	Backpack	32
8/31/17	CVS	Glucose meter, strips & lancets	20
9/1/17	Flea Market	Caregiver Uniform	32
9/1/17	PCMS	Medical Gloves	8
9/1/17	Walmart	White under-uniform T-shirts	8
		TOTAL	$317

CHAPTER 7: SWEET MEMORIES

Of course things weren't always doom and gloom between *Aileen* and me. Despite the occasional war of words, we tried to make the best of the moment. We sometimes joked around, increased intimacy, danced together, watched TV, went to the movies, parks, Dave & Busters, the community pool, the beach, restaurants, the gym etc. We visited *Ate Nelia* once a week to watch DVD movies and order Chinese food. We also enjoyed playing one of my board games called **Bezique**. She liked it a lot and it was often a stress reliever.

Although she couldn't cook my favorite dishes, she'd often cook Filipino food or the usual rice, fish and vegetables. She enjoyed going out for **shawarma** *(Arabic Wrap)* at the food court of *Coral Square Mall*. It reminded her of the time she spent in the *UAE*.

She once saved a shirt I was about throw away by cutting out the arms making it sleeveless; allowing me to wear it to bed as pajamas. She would pick flowers outside in the morning and put them in pots and water them everyday on our balcony. She helped me pick out, move and arrange free furniture we got from our condo association. And whenever it was appropriate, we would do a dumpster dive when we saw good items that others were getting rid of in the community. *Aileen* is not flashy, conceited or too demanding.

Some of her blunders included burning some meat on the stove, accidentally walking into a glass sliding door, using too much bleach when cleaning causing her temporary trouble breathing, being a bit slow in understanding some things, mostly due I think, to the language barrier. But despite the blunders and lack of compatibility in other areas, I appreciated that she left her family behind to be with me. She seemed willing to go through thick and thin, even in what appeared to be an uncertain future. She would look to me for reassurance but often didn't know how to express it. At times I thought she had the mentality of a twelve-year old. In fact, one of the managers in our community, jokingly said, that she acts like a little girl. Maybe that's why I felt the need to protect her.

I tried to understand her concerns and frustrations and did the best I could to limit the stress she was under. Stress, because we often talked about her possibly going back home. And although I was watching my budget, I always offered to take her out to eat and do other things. She liked when I massage her with sensual oil and she would sometimes massage me as well. She likes when I hold her tight; saying when I do, she feels safe! Whenever I was dealing with other issues, she seemed to listen and offered encouragement. Although we often differed on how to solve certain problems.

We played the powerball lottery a couple of times. And because finances were tight, you can imagine the anticipation of winning a jackpot. It would've had a big impact on our plans. *Aileen* made a habit of picking up pennies, coins on the streets. It wasn't much but it gave her a feeling of having something since she wasn't working. But from time to time, I'd also give her some allowance money for whatever she wanted; including sending money back home.

Whenever we'd go out, she'd always take pictures of the American Flag when she sees it; perhaps a reminder of being in America. We sometimes prayed together, especially before a meal. She cleaned, did the laundry and helped in rearranging furniture in the house. We had a washer and dryer next door. But sometimes she would wash by hand in the tub and hang the clothes to dry on the balcony. That's usually how laundry is done in the Philippines AND in Haiti for that matter.

Aileen had never driven in her life. So it wasn't easy trying to teach her how to drive. Especially with my car being a stick shift. She could never get used to it and would fear or hesitate if she thought I was being impatient. The air conditioner in my car wasn't working. So when we went out on hot days, she'd put a towel over her head and we'd patiently ride the heat together. Once, we went to Lakeland in central Florida for a weekend. I rented a car that was more comfortable than mine with a working AC. Lakeland was an ideal place to teach her how to drive. She enjoyed circling around the many lakes there. She was still uncomfortable behind the wheel, but did much better than in my car. Since my home in Lakeland was rented, we slept in the car at a large Walmart parking lot. In the morning we'd go to a local planet fitness to use the bathroom and do a little workout. Even though sleeping in the car was uncomfortable, it was fun. We made the most of it and *Aileen* was very helpful. On the way back home, we did some sightseeing, dined at a restaurant and took pictures at Disney World.

CHAPTER 8: BITTER SEPARATION

Given all that had transpired between us. I didn't feel ready to commit at this time. We agreed we needed to give each other space. We even talked about finding our soulmates. I wanted someone I could better communicate with. Someone less jealous and more sensitive to my needs. I was also a bit concerned about where I was financially. And if she got sick, her medical cost would be out of my reach, even if I added her to my insurance. We talked about her returning to the Philippines; and depending on how things go, we could try a different approach. And although painful, a separation under the circumstances could possibly bring us closer later on.

I worried because of the old saying **Out of sight, out of mind**. But I was encouraged by another saying: **Absence makes the heart grow fonder.** And to me the business was our ticket to being reunited. I told her we had a date with *Aileen Cares* and I looked forward to working with her on it. With today's technology we can easily share files and photos over the internet.

So after getting the equipment for *Aileen Cares* along with some clothes and other items for her family, I made reservations for her for 7 p.m. on September 6, 2017. And although *Aileen* seemed less worried about going back, it was not easy. She'd turn to me in bed and say "Goodbye po!" She'd also tell me to keep my **Titi** *(Tagalog for **Penis**)* to myself! Yea, she does have a sense of humor that I am thankful for. At times, it's a stress reliever and reassures me that somehow she was going to be OK.

Hurricane Irma

Maybe this was a coincidence, but the reservation coincided with **Irma**; a major category-5 hurricane warning for south Florida. That seemed to speed up the urgency to move things along because we weren't sure if we'd still have a home after that. And although *Aileen* might not admit, after about six months in the U.S., I think she was looking forward to seeing her family again.

Delayed Period

As if the pressure wasn't bad enough, *Aileen*'s period was close to a week late☹. For her age, she's had a fairly regular menstrual cycle. Since she'd been in the U.S. her symptoms had even improved. She had less headaches, didn't throw up as much and her blood seemed clearer. However, a couple of days before her scheduled flight, she told me she threw up in the morning. She said she was OK with leaving, but because she wasn't feeling well, she wasn't up to the long flight. I suspected there was nothing to worry about because I don't remember putting anything inside her during intimacy. But you never know; accidents do happen. At least that's what she was thinking. I was terrified! We were already having money and relationship issues and a pregnancy would REALLY complicate things.

That caused me to put a little more pressure on her to leave. I know it sounds horrible! I still cringe at the thought of it today. It wasn't fair to put her in that position. But I thought because we couldn't make things work in the U.S., I could always send money to care for a baby, IF she was truly pregnant. On the other hand, it would also be terrible: not only would she not have gotten her papers, she'd be returning home with a baby! How would that look to her family and friends back home? But thank God, her period came fully on the **same day** she was scheduled to leave. By then, she was also feeling much better and with a positive attitude.

Pocket Money

When we talked about pocket money, I wasn't too happy with her asking for $1,000. I guess she thought I was to blame for everything and put a price on it. I already had a lot on my plate and we had previously discussed how much I would give her and what it might be used for:

- $300 towards *Aileen Cares*
- $200 towards **ukay-ukay** (*Filipino: second-hand apparels such as clothes, bags, shoes etc.*) to buy and sell for a profit
- $200 towards moving into a nicer efficiency in her community
- $100 for her kids
- $60 pocket money for the trip.

The above is in addition to clothes and other gifts we bought for her and her family.

At The Airport

It was raining that day because we were already getting the outer bands of hurricane *Irma*. But we did make it safely to the Airport. I got permission to wait with *Aileen* at the gate. We had at least two hours before her flight so we spent the time talking and planning. I felt terrible having to let her go, but this seemed like the right thing to do. We still had mixed feelings but reminded ourselves we would soon be working together with *Aileen Cares*. We shared a large burger and soda for lunch and snapped a couple of pictures. But we didn't eat much. *Aileen* said her stomach was in a knot.

Her first Airline was *Virgin America*. And as we got closer to boarding time, I could hear her groaning softly; something she does at times to express sadness or anxiety. When they began the call for passengers to board the plane, We both tried to hold back our tears. We hugged and kissed each other goodbye. She got in line, clenching her face as she continued trying to be strong. She wouldn't look at me even though I was blowing kisses and waving goodbye. **But as she got closer and closer to the boarding gate, she turned and looked at me☺.** I'll never forget that moment!

After she got on, I waited for a long while. The plane was in a long line for departure so I went outside. And as I was getting in my car, I finally saw *Virgin America* take off. And **Just like that, *Aileen* was gone!** I could only imagine how broken she was inside the plane. I was sad too, but also relieved at the same time. We both were under a lot of stress: Back and forth on things we couldn't agree on; not to mention the issues related to adjusting her status.

Because *Aileen* didn't have enough space for everything, I promised to later ship her a box. In it, I'd also put a small white color TV with built-in radio we'd gotten from a friend in the community. Aileen really liked that TV. So I made sure I put it safely in the box together with a few essentials, personal items and some clothes she was leaving behind. I sent the box on October 31, 2017. It arrived in Manila about three months later.

Timeline Of Events

DATE	EVENT
August 11, 2015	Meeting *Aileen* on Filipino Cupid
January 21 to February 9, 2016	Visit to the Philippines to see *Aileen*
March - June 2016 petition	Back in the U.S. from the Philippines
June 2016 - March 28 2017	From filing the petition to *Aileen*'s travel to the U.S.
March 29, 2017 - September 6, 2017	*Aileen*'s time in the U.S.
September 6, 2017	*Aileen* returns to the Philippines
September 8, 2017 - Present Day	Continued occasional chats with *Aileen*

CHAPTER 9: BITTER COST

Embarking on this journey is not to be taken lightly. It carries heavy emotional and financial consequences. Usually the petitioner is expected to pay for ALL related expenses until the fiancé can work and contribute. Some consider it an investment. But it can be a risky investment if you're not careful. That's not to say I didn't have feelings for *Aileen*. I did and still do. And despite the trials, my emotions grew and I found myself loving her more and more.

Below, I've outlined the approximate cost for the privilege of bringing *Aileen* to the U.S. My experience was cut short but I've included ALL the expenses you can expect to face. Money you spend on your fiancé and vacation related expenses are not included:

DESCRIPTION	FORMS	COST ($U.S.)
Initial Petition		$340
- Main application *(includes K-2 declaration)*	I-129F	
- E-Notification of Acceptance	G-1145	
- Biographic Information *(one from each of you)*	G-325A	
- Affidavit of Support	I-134	
- Statement of Intent to Marry *(one from each of you)*		
- Notice of Action	I-797	
Passport photos, certified mail etc...		25
Plane Ticket to meet *Aileen* in Manila		1,192
Car Rental in Manila		240
Hotel Rental		346
National Visa Center *(application for interview in Manila)*	DS-160	255
Medical Exam		245
Police Clearances and other legal issues *(if applicable)*		205
Aileen's one-way ticket to the U.S.		1,000
Wedding Dress		0
Wedding Ring		0
Adjustment of Status	I-485	1,070
- Affidavit of Support	I-864	
Employment Authorization	I-765	495
Advance Parole *(optional)*	I-131	575
Return ticket to the Philippines		790
Pocket money to *Aileen*		860
Aileen-Cares Equipment		315
Box sent to *Aileen* after her return trip		125

The items listed in red are things left undone because *Aileen* went back to the Philippines. The **main application** *(I-129F)* is the starting point of the fiancé visa process. There's a K-2 section where I had named *Aileen*'s daughter. The k-2 allows children of the K-1 petition to obtain a visa under the same application. The K-2 beneficiary must be under 21. My understanding is that once you and your fiancé are married and you've applied for adjustment of status *(I-485)* the child can contact the National Visa Center at the U.S. Embassy and begin the K-2 process. *Aileen*'s daughter would have had to undergo some of the steps she went through, including a medical exam. This means you could anticipate additional costs in connection to this process. The electronic notification acceptance *(G-1145)* is a short, optional form you can include to request a text message and/or email when USCIS accepts the petition.

Aileen and I had to include the Biographic Information form *(G-325A)*. It's a painstaking task of including all places you've lived and worked, for the most recent five years. The initial affidavit of support *(I-134)* is an assessment of your finances showing that you have the means to take care of your fiancé. I don't even think it was looked at when *Aileen* went for her interview. The one you really need to be concerned with, as I've said, is form *I-864* when you adjust status. Had everything gone right, *Aileen* would have been eligible to apply for citizenship in just three years since I'm a citizen. It normally takes five years.

The notice of action form *(I-797)* is the reply I received from USCIS stating that my petition had been approved. It also said that it was being sent to the *National Visa Center* for processing and to direct further inquiries to that department. If there are any issues, they'll send you a notice of action stating what the problem is. I did have to clear up some things related to my mailing address. After that, I got the final notice of approval. The employment authorization form *(I-765)* would have allowed *Aileen* to legally work in the U.S., while the adjustment of status is under review. The optional advance-parole form *(I-131)* would have allowed her to travel outside the U.S. while waiting for the green card.

CHAPTER 10: BITTER DISTANCE

Aileen and I continued to chat on and off after she went back to the Philippines. I talked to her between flights. We both knew we would feel the impact of the decision after she left. But that was just the beginning.

Loneliness

When she first got back she told me how she felt sooo alone and empty inside! She was back in the same tiny room where we chatted numerous times. I know she would be heartbroken and I tried to comfort her as much as I could. There were regrets and uncertainties as we found ourselves confused and alone again, separated by many miles of ocean. She said to me one time in a chat **"Mahal, I come back?"** Perhaps it hadn't yet dawn on her that we lost the opportunity that would have given her a better life in the U.S. I could go on with my own life of course; but despite the trials, I still felt the need to care and provide for her. After all, she's still my wife.

Atelophobia

I hoped that *Aileen* and I could learn to understand and trust each other more. Sometimes, we'd discuss her coming back if things improve. But she was angry and fearful of the idea. It took me a while, but I came to realize that this may have to do with a condition called **Atelophobia** *(fear of imperfection)*. You see, *Aileen* began to think that she was not good enough for me in the U.S. She felt rejected, isolated and unsociable with my family and friends. Instead, she found refuge in her own family back home. She said she'll stay knowing her family loves her. According to her, if I really loved her I wouldn't have let her go. Her family seem to share the same view and advise her to stop talking to me. But so far she's not taken that advice seriously.

Aileen Cares

When she first got back, *Aileen* was happy with her new gadgets and began to charge some friends for basic services. She made some quick cash with her glucose meter and digital blood pressure machine. Little by little, I thought she could focus on finding new patients and then split salaries with other caregivers looking for work. She could do it on the side while working a full-time job. Soon after she got back, she did find a job caring for an elderly woman 24/7 in a hospital. But the time began to weigh her down. And about a month later, the family's plan for the patient had changed. *Aileen* was offered to continue caring for her at a nursing home. But the place was too far so she turned it down.

In the past, I've made some comments about her lack of willingness to work. For that she always takes a defensive approach whenever we talk about it. She says I accuse her of being lazy. But *Aileen Cares* was the one thing I thought would change that. Now she gets upset whenever I bring up the business or anything job related. She later thought of going to work in Japan or Qatar. She's even contacted an agency about it but so far has not yet committed.

After a while, she gave up on *Aileen Cares* altogether; saying the people are poor and didn't want to pay. I said it would not be easy but she should continue to share her business cards. With more experience, others would begin to call on her for services. I explained that all businesses face some challenges at first. But out of the blue, she started accusing me of wanting her to do the business to give ME money! What ever gave her that idea? Maybe I was asking too much of her. She's not business minded and didn't seem motivated at all to follow through on the plans we had made. Now she's back to working on and off as a caregiver whenever an agency calls. In doing so she blames me for being back to taking *jeepneys* in the hot sun and in the same polluted environment.

Same Old, Same Old

Not much has changed since *Aileen* left. We continue to chat; sometimes daily. She still accuses me of being unfaithful, curses me in text chats, shows me pictures of my ex-girlfriend, threatens to send my naked pictures to friends on Messenger, says I pushed her back home and destroyed her life, calls me a liar because "I promised to change her life," asks if I just wanted to f*** her. She's also asked me to divorce her. I have thought about filing for divorce, but so far have not followed through on it.

The communication barrier seems just as strong between us. She has a huge temper and jealousy issues. When she cools off after an argument and I get upset, she says to me "you don't know me by now?" In other words, she can go on an emotional roller coaster then expects me to pamper her. I've also been concerned about her apparent vindictive nature. To me that's not good if you marry someone who's already giving evidence of possibly becoming your Ex someday!

Declined Health

When *Aileen* was in the U.S., she gained close to seven pounds. Her menstrual symptoms had improved. She had some occasional back pain but her overall health seemed good. About three months after she got back, she came down with a case of *Urinary Tract Infection (UTI)* and was coughing a lot. She seems to have lost weight; but says it's because she's cut back on rice and other unhealthy foods. She was treated quickly and inexpensively in the Philippines and has since been recovering. But I do get emotional when I see her face on video. I'm afraid the experience has really taken a toll on her as her face already looks a bit older and thinner.

Uncertain Future

For now, *Aileen* and I are still married and she didn't violate any laws on her visa. Assuming things improve between us, financially and otherwise, it should be easier if we decided to do this again. It's possible her love for me is sincere. I mean, why else would she openly express negative feelings towards me at the expense of losing everything?

Occasionally we both browse other dating sites in the hope of finding our soulmates. So far, nothing serious from either side. She says she's had interest from men, who've offered her a better life but that she's not interested. She'd like to move on, but finds it hard to let go. I continue to have a certain weakness for her as well. Maybe it's sadness on my part. I had unfriended her on Facebook for her jealous behavior; I thought it might help her to trust me. But it doesn't seem to matter anyway because she doesn't have much of a profile on Facebook anymore.

She's filled with hate for me and says she needs to forget and move on. Maybe I should stop talking to her; because until I can fully commit, I don't want to give her hopes and add to her grief. Even if we talk about plans of taking a vacation somewhere or me spending time with her in Manila, she questions what happens after, and I can't give her a straight answer.

Right now, I'm not sure what the future holds for us. It's been eight months since *Aileen* left and she still seems **traumatized** by the experience. And I see her everywhere I go; in the house and the places where we used to go. It's like she marked her territory so that I would purposely miss her. But it's more a feeling of missed connection and what might have been. A sad moment that begs the question: *"How did she miss out on an opportunity that meant so much to her? How did we end up here?"*

Maybe we just have to accept the fact that we're not right for each other. But I continue praying and hoping that God will either bring us together again someday or help us find CLOSURE!

A WORD TO THE WISE

Once again, this book is not meant to discourage anyone because not everyone will have the same experience. However, the information I've offered could help you avoid some pitfalls. I doubt I'll ever go through this again. It doesn't mean I'll never date another Filipina. I would simply be more careful in the future. Hopefully you will too if you ever decide to take the 90-Day challenge.

Thank you for reading my story. I've put together a Facebook Page at *facebook.com/bittersweet90days*. Please LIKE to receive updates. Your questions and feedback are welcome, whether good OR bad. Also feel free to share your own experience and let us know what you would have done differently if you were *Dantes* or *Aileen*.

THE VISA PROCESS

PERSON	PROCESS	FORM
	COUPLE meets 2 years prior and gathers proof of relationship. Engagement not necessary.	N/A
	PETITIONER - MAN OR WOMAN files. Average time may vary.	I-129 / 1145 / G-325A / I-134
USCIS	USCIS reviews petition package. May ask for more information known as *(request for evidence - REF)*. Average time: 3 to 6 months.	N/A
	NATIONAL VISA CENTER *(NVC)* reviews case and performs background checks. NVC Forwards case to U.S. Embassy where fiancé is. Petitioner receives notice of action *(I-797)*. Average time: 1 month.	I-797
EMBASSY	U.S. EMBASSY ABROAD receives and processes the case. Sends K-1 packet and visa application to fiancé. Petitioner receives copies. Average time: 1 - 2 weeks.	N/A
Fiancé	FIANCÉ files DS-160, reviews checklist and gathers ALL documents including police clearances. DS-160 can be filed online. Petitioner provides I-134 *(affidavit of support)* Average time: 1 - 4 weeks.	DS-160 / I-134

FIANCÉ gather proofs of relationship including pictures and chats. Good idea to make an album. Fiancé OR Embassy may set a date for interview. Average time: 2 - 6 weeks.	N/A
MEDICAL EXAM. Fiancé schedules & receives medical exam from approved physician. Physician provides sealed results to Fiancé or Embassy. Average time: 1 - 3 weeks.	N/A
VISA INTERVIEW. Fiancé brings K-1 packet and ALL documents. Embassy checks eligibility and all documents. Visa approval is communicated at a later time. Average time: 1 day.	N/A
VISA ISSUED. Fiancé works out how to receive Visa from the Embassy. Visa valid for six months. K-2 visa may be issued later. Embassy provides packet with sealed medical report. Average time: up to 1 month.	N/A
Fiancé TRAVELS TO U.S. with K-2 children if any. Fiancé presents sealed medical packet to customs and obtains I-94.	N/A
Couple GETS MARRIED legally and obtains marriage certificate. Time Limit: 90 days from date on I-94.	N/A
Petitioner ADJUSTS STATUS. I-485, affidavit of support (I-864), optional employment authorization (I-765). Optional advanced parole (I-131) allows spouse to travel. Average time: several months.	I-485 / I-864 / I-765 / I-131
Petitioner files for SOCIAL SECURITY for Fiancé. Average time: 1 week.	SS-5
USCIS issues a 2-year CONDITIONAL GREEN CARD. Spouse can formally work and travel. Average time may vary.	N/A
REMOVE CONDITIONS. During the 2-year conditional, gather proof of bona-fide marriage. File I-751 with USCIS. Prepare for possible interview of both of you.	I-751
Spouse receives a **10-YEAR GREEN CARD**. Renew when necessary.	N/A

www.ingramcontent.com/pod-product-compliance
Lightning Source LLC
Chambersburg PA
CBHW060951050426
42453CB00009B/1152